W9-DES-556

BLOOMFIELD TOWNSHIP PUBLIC LIBRARY

3 1160 00546 1160

BLOOMFIELD TOWNSHIP PUBLIC LIBRARY
1099 Lone Pine Road
Bloomfield Hills, Michigan 48302-2410

SPORTS INJURIES:
HOW TO PREVENT, DIAGNOSE, & TREAT

FOOTBALL

Sports Injuries:
How to Prevent, Diagnose, & Treat

- Baseball
- Basketball
- Cheerleading
- Equestrian
- Extreme Sports
- Field
- Field Hockey
- Football
- Gymnastics
- Hockey
- Ice Skating
- Lacrosse
- Soccer
- Track
- Volleyball
- Weight Training
- Wrestling

SPORTS INJURIES:
HOW TO PREVENT, DIAGNOSE, & TREAT

FOOTBALL

JOHN WRIGHT

BLOOMFIELD TOWNSHIP PUBLIC LIBRARY
1099 Lone Pine Road
Bloomfield Hills, Michigan 48302-2410

MASON CREST PUBLISHERS
www.masoncrest.com

Mason Crest Publishers Inc.
370 Reed Road
Broomall, PA 19008
(866) MCP-BOOK (toll free)
www.masoncrest.com

Copyright © 2004 Mason Crest Publishers, Inc.

All rights reserved. No part of this publication may be reproduced or transmitted in any form or by any means, electronic or mechanical, including photocopying, recording, taping, or any information storage and retrieval system, without permission in writing from the publisher.

First printing

1 2 3 4 5 6 7 8 9 10

Library of Congress Cataloging-in-Publication Data on file
at the Library of Congress

ISBN 1-59084-632-X

Series ISBN 1-59084-625-7

Editorial and design by
Amber Books Ltd.
Bradley's Close
74–77 White Lion Street
London N1 9PF
www.amberbooks.co.uk

Project Editor: Michael Spilling
Design: Graham Curd
Picture Research: Natasha Jones

Printed and bound in the Hashemite Kingdom of Jordan

PICTURE CREDITS
Corbis: 6, 8, 10, 11, 12, 13, 15, 17, 18, 20, 22, 23, 24, 26, 28, 29, 31, 34, 36, 38, 39, 40, 42, 48, 50, 52, 54, 55, 56, 58.

FRONT COVER: All Corbis.

ILLUSTRATIONS: Courtesy of Amber Books except:
Bright Star Publishing plc: 43, 45, 46.

IMPORTANT NOTICE
This book is intended to provide general information about sports injuries, their prevention, and their treatment. The information contained herein is not intended as a substitute for professional medical care. Always consult a doctor before beginning any exercise program, and for diagnosis and treatment of any injury. Accordingly, the publisher cannot accept any responsibility for any prosecution or proceedings brought or instituted against any person or body as a result of the use or misuse of the techniques and information within.

CONTENTS

Foreword   6

History   8

Mental Preparations   18

Warming Up and Conditioning to Avoid Injuries   26

Equipment   34

Common Injuries and Treatment   40

Careers in Football   52

Glossary   60

Further Information   62

Index   64

MAR 16 2004

Foreword

Sports Injuries: How to Prevent, Diagnose, and Treat is a seventeen-volume series written for young people who are interested in learning about various sports and how to participate in them safely. Each volume examines the history of the sport and the rules of play; it also acts as a guide for prevention and treatment of injuries, and includes instruction on stretching, warming up, and strength training, all of which can help players avoid the most common musculoskeletal injuries. *Sports Injuries* offers ways for readers to improve their performance and gain more enjoyment from playing sports, and young athletes will find these volumes informative and helpful in their pursuit of excellence.

Sports medicine professionals assigned to a sport that they are not familiar with can also benefit from this series. For example, a football athletic trainer may need to provide medical care for a local gymnastics meet. Although the emergency medical principles and action plan would remain the same, the athletic trainer could provide better care for the gymnasts after reading a simple overview of the principles of gymnastics in *Sports Injuries*.

Although these books offer an overview, they are not intended to be comprehensive in the recognition and management of sports injuries. The text helps the reader appreciate and gain awareness of the common injuries possible during participation in sports. Reference material and directed readings are provided for those who want to delve further into the subject.

Written in a direct and easily accessible style, *Sports Injuries* is an enjoyable series that will help young people learn about sports and sports medicine.

Susan Saliba, Ph.D., National Athletic Trainers' Association Education Council

Action at the Rose Bowl often has the crowd on their feet in Pasadena, California.

History

With such colorful additions as cheerleaders, marching bands, and college homecoming ceremonies, football is America's most spectacular team sport. Each year, nearly two million athletes are attracted to the gridiron, in order to play a game dating from the nineteenth century.

Football developed in the United States from the English games of football (soccer) and rugby, brought across the Atlantic in the 1820s. Colleges along the East Coast were the first to import the game, which was so rough that Harvard banned football in 1860. The rules of the early game seem strange today. A team had three **downs** to make five yards (five meters) for a first down, which is why the modern **gridiron** is marked off in five-yard sections. Players could not tackle a runner below the waist. And a touchdown was worth only two points, a conversion added four more, and a field goal was five points.

This exciting game quickly spread across the country, adopted by the University of Michigan in 1870 and by Washington & Lee in 1873. The Rose Bowl, the first post-season "bowl" matchup between top teams, began in 1902.

The forward pass was introduced in 1906 by John Heisman, whose name is now on the famous Heisman Trophy, which is awarded annually to the best college player of the year. More innovations quickly followed. Another exciting play was the "flying wedge" formation, which let the receiver of a **kickoff** be

Red Grange, a halfback for the University of Illinois, played for the Chicago Bears from 1925 to 1934. He was nicknamed the "Galloping Ghost" because he was hard to tackle.

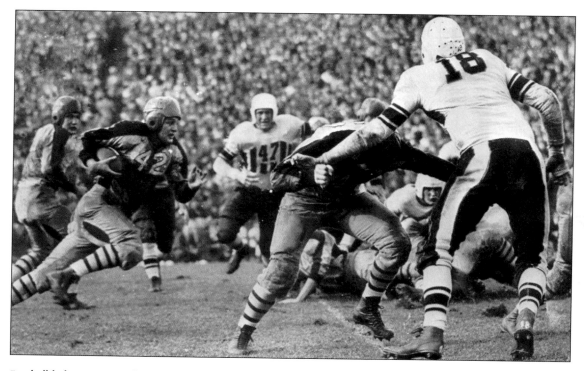

Football helmets were softer in the first half of the twentieth century. In this 1938 college game, Columbia's Sid Luckman charges into the Colgate line.

surrounded by a tight wedge of large blockers, who stormed toward the kickoff team. This formation injured many players and even caused some deaths. After President Theodore Roosevelt complained, it was banned in 1910.

By the 1920s, plays were similar to those used today. The big difference between football of the 1920s and modern football was in clothing and equipment: the padded uniforms looked baggy, and players wore snug leather helmets that resembled those worn by early pilots and offered poor protection. Some players even refused to wear the helmets because they considered them unmanly.

These were the years of Notre Dame's legendary coach Knute Rockne and his famous backfield made up of the "Four Horsemen." It was also the time period in

BASIC FOOTBALL RULES

Each team has eleven players on the field, divided into the offensive, defensive, and specialist teams. A game is divided into quarters; play lasts for sixty minutes for college and professional games, and forty-eight minutes for high school games. Timeouts make the game last much longer.

Points are scored in four different ways: six points for a touchdown; three for a field goal; two for a safety (when the ball carrier is tackled or grounds the ball behind his own goal line because a tackle is not needed if the ball carrier falls to the ground); and either one or two for a conversion. If kicked, a conversion will earn one point, although a college team will earn two points if it successfully runs or passes from the three-yard line (a pro team earns one point by running or passing from the two-yard line). After a kickoff, the offensive team has four plays to advance ten yards for a first down and begin the series again. If the offensive team fails to make a first down, they punt to the other team, which then begins its offensive series. The offense can also lose the ball by a fumble or intercepted pass. If a team scores, they kick off to their opponents.

The basic game is the same, but football has undergone many important rule changes through the years.

which professional football in America took off: in 1920, eleven teams organized as the American Professional Football Association. Their names, including the Dayton Triangles and the Massillon Tigers, would hardly be recognized today, although the Decatur Staleys became the Chicago Bears in 1922. That same year, the American Professional Football Association was renamed the National Football League (NFL).

FOOTBALL GOES NATIONAL

By the middle of the twentieth century, the modern game as we know it today was in place. Fans around the nation could watch televised games between championship teams such as the New York Giants, Cleveland Browns, Philadelphia Eagles, and Dallas Cowboys. In 1967, the first Super Bowl took place: the Green Bay Packers,

Green Bay Packers give their coach, Vince Lombardi, the traditional victory ride after defeating the Los Angeles Rams in 1960 for the NFL's Western Division title.

coached by Vince Lombardi, defeated the Kansas City Chiefs, a team from the American Football League (AFL), which was formed in 1960. These two leagues merged in 1970, keeping the NFL name.

By 2002, expansion had increased the NFL to thirty-one teams. At the same time, college football was also going strong, led by such successful coaches as Alabama's Paul "Bear" Bryant, Nebraska's Tom Osborne, Penn State's Joe Paterno, Florida State's Bobby Bowden, and Grambling State's Eddie Robinson in Louisiana.

The forward pass, introduced in 1906, is an exciting play. Originally, an incompleted pass drew a 15-yard (13.7-m) penalty.

RULES OF FAIR PLAY

Throughout football's history, more and more rules have been introduced to protect the players. Although some penalties, such as offside, are there to assure fair play, many rules and penalties were devised to prevent dangerous actions. The fair catch violation, for instance, protects a receiver of a punt or kickoff as he stands helpless, looking up for the ball. If he waves his hand in the air, he cannot be touched by the rushing players.

Other illegal plays include grabbing a player's face mask, which could cause a serious neck injury; roughing the passer or kicker by hitting him after he no longer has the ball; clipping, as this illegal hard hit from behind can seriously damage the knees or back; spearing, in which a player drives his helmet into a downed opponent; piling on after a tackle; and unsportsmanlike conduct, which covers overly aggressive action, including fights. These are only a few of the many regulations that have been introduced to avoid injuries.

PLAYING SURFACES

Injuries are also affected by the type of playing-field surface. A lot of ground has to be covered in a football game, as the length of the field, including the two end zones, is 120 yards (110 m), and the width is 160 feet (488 m).

Artificial grass was first developed to respond to the needs of players in another sport, baseball. In 1966, the Houston Astrodome opened, but its grass surface died after panels in its transparent dome were painted to help baseball players see fly balls. A synthetic turf was laid (nylon grass over a concrete base) and named AstroTurf. It was cheaper to keep up, as there was no grass to cut and no holes to repair.

Not surprisingly, football teams soon began to consider using artificial playing fields. Among the first teams to do so were the Seattle Seahawks, the University of Nebraska, and the University of Washington. There have been some problems, however, with this change of playing surface. Players complain of "turf burn" when they fall and skid on "the rug." Others blame knee and toe injuries on the artificial surface because it does not have the "give" of real earth. And when a player slides, artificial turf tends to grab his shoes. In 1996, a survey of 965 NFL players revealed that ninety-six percent thought AstroTurf caused more injuries than grass.

The makers of AstroTurf have responded to these criticisms, improving the product's padding and shock-absorbing layers. Other artificial playing surfaces have also been developed. One called FieldTurf became available in 1999. This has a softer cushion than dirt because a blend of sand and ground rubber pieces

THE ULTIMATE WINNER

Described by *Sports Illustrated* as "the ultimate winner," Joe Montana looked fragile for a quarterback. But he led Notre Dame to the national championship in 1977, and later took his San Francisco 49ers to four Super Bowls, winning them all. He also became the only player to be named the Super Bowl's "Most Valuable Player" three times. What made him great was his coolness in do-or-die situations. In thirty-one games, he led his team to come-from-behind victories in the fourth quarter, earning him the title of "the comeback kid."

Montana also had to come back from critical injuries. When he threw a pass in the 1986 season opener, he suffered a ruptured disk and underwent a two-hour operation. Advised to give up football, he was back on the field two months later, throwing touchdown passes.

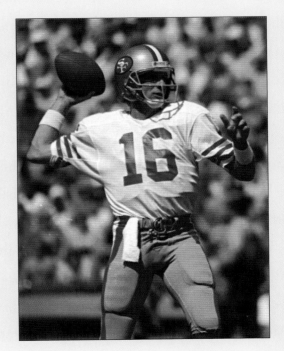

When Montana retired in 1994, his statistics were awesome: 273 passing touchdowns; 3,409 completions; and total passing yardage of 40,551 yards.

Joe Montana was captain of the San Francisco 49ers when they won the Super Bowl in 1982, 1985, 1989, and 1990.

are packed around each blade of "grass." Another, called AstroPlay, uses a rubber cushioning without the sand to give players an even softer landing. This is important because dangerous injuries may occur to the head, brain, neck, and spine when a player's head strikes the turf at a high speed.

By 2002, four pro football teams—Dallas, Detroit, Philadelphia, and Seattle—had artificial playing fields. That same year, almost 200 schools in the United States chose to lay it for their teams.

FOOTBALL GREATS

Brooklyn-born Vince Lombardi (1913–1970) became one of America's most successful football coaches. "Winning isn't everything," he said. "It's the only thing." Indeed, it became so for the Green Bay Packers, the team that Lombardi coached from 1959 to 1968. In that time, he led the Packers through freezing winters in their Wisconsin stadium to take the conference title six times, the NFL title five times, and, to top his career, the first two Super Bowls, in 1967 and 1968. He retired in 1968, but returned a year later to coach the Washington Redskins to their first winning record in fourteen years.

Players remember this famous coach for being tough, but always fair. Lombardi demanded dedication to the game and to himself. In return, he gave players his respect and friendship, inspiring them to become champions. In 1971, Lombardi was inducted into the Professional Football Hall of Fame, and the Super Bowl championship trophy was named the Vince Lombardi Super Bowl Trophy. In 2000, the ESPN television network named him "Coach of the Century."

Alabama's great coach Paul "Bear" Bryant was a larger-than-life personality who earned his nickname as a teenager in Arkansas by wrestling a carnival bear for money. He played on the undefeated 1934 Alabama team, then coached at

Maryland, Kentucky, and Texas A. & M., before returning to Alabama to take over the Crimson Tide. From 1958 to 1982, he took the Tide to six national championships, thirteen Southeastern Conference titles, and twenty-four straight bowl games. "My favorite play," Bryant once said, "is the one where the player pitches the ball back to the official after scoring a touchdown." Bryant ended his career as the most successful coach ever for a major college, with 323 victories to his name. The annual award for the College Football Coach of the Year is now called The Bear Bryant Award.

Bryant expected his players to give more than 100 percent effort and to obey his rules. A sign in his office said, "Be good or be gone." He was known equally as well for instructing his players to act and dress like gentlemen. After flooring an opponent with a crushing tackle, an Alabama player was expected to hold out a hand to help him up. "I have tried to teach them to show class, to have pride, and to display character," he said. "I think football—winning games—takes care of itself if you do that."

"Bear" Bryant was on the 1935 Alabama team that won the Rose Bowl over Stanford. He later coached the Tide to a record twenty-four straight bowl games.

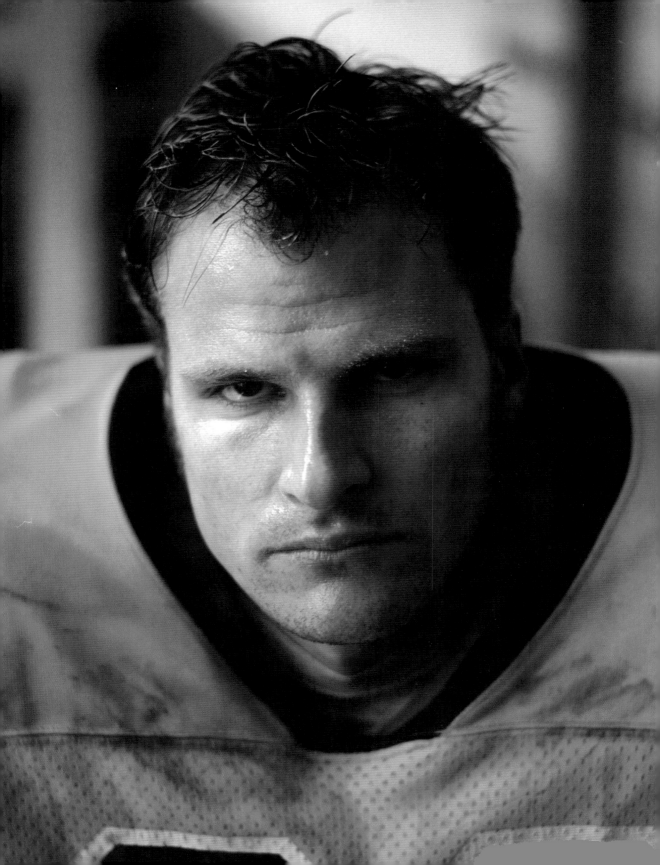

Mental Preparations

"Teams do not go physically flat," noted coach Vincent Lombardi. "They go mentally stale." This sums up what all coaches know about the values of motivation, concentration, and mental discipline.

Mental preparation and motivation play an important part in sports. For instance, a coach might challenge players by pinning negative newspaper comments about the team on their bulletin board. This has often been used to "fire up" players to win. Or, in a more personal mental preparation, you might be a lineman who must take on an All-State player in the next game. In that case, a good pregame strategy would be to visualize over and over the quick moves you will make to overcome your opponent's power and avoid injuries. This is like watching a video of your performance in advance.

Sports psychologists call this "mental imagery." As the brain rules the body, a person can actually perform better by first seeing his performance happening in his mind. This is what occurs when a player gets "psyched up" by thinking of the excitement of an upcoming game. Remember that attitudes can be controlled. An especially important attitude enhancer is to keep a positive self-image. Research shows that negative thinking often leads to injuries, so negative thoughts should be immediately replaced by positive ones. Assure yourself that you will play safely and be in control on the field, doing your best and having fun. Focus on changes

"Relaxed attention" is often seen on the faces of players (here, Paul Hornung) during a game. This is one of the confidence-building techniques that can help players to perform well and avoid injuries.

you can make to improve your performance. If, however, you adopt a "win at all costs" attitude, injuries may follow.

Players also perform better and more safely if they reduce anxiety. This involves controlling your attitudes and emotions, which will increase concentration and confidence. Remember that your opponents are as anxious as you are. Find time to relax and picture yourself successfully catching a pass, making a tackle, or doing whatever other play is necessary during the game.

Relaxation and confidence-building techniques can be done after a pregame

The agony of defeat can quickly be erased by the next victory. Mental exercises can help a player through the bad days and build his self-confidence.

warm-up to help lower muscular tension. They can even be practiced while playing because it is possible to feel calm and positive when you are energized. This is why we sometimes see players calmly talking to themselves during a game; it is called "relaxed attention." Injuries are less common when anger and anxiety are controlled. If a player is too emotional on the field, high levels of adrenaline can cause muscle tension and injury. The Fitness & Sports Medicine Center at the famous Mayo Clinic in Rochester, Minnesota, emphasizes the importance of being in **the zone**—the state when your mind and body are working calmly together for the best results.

AIM HIGH

Mental imagery is linked to setting goals. A kicker might promise himself to average forty yards in a game, or a quarterback's goal may be a pass-completion rate of seventy percent. You can use the same technique. Be confident that you can meet the challenge. Motivate yourself still more by telling others what you are trying to do. A famous example of this was when Babe Ruth pointed to the outfield fence in the 1932 World Series, then proceeded to hit a home run over that same fence. Another example occurred when Joe Namath, the star New York Jets quarterback, publicly "guaranteed" that his AFL champions would defeat the highly favored NFL champion Baltimore Colts in the 1969 Super Bowl III. Namath was hobbled by serious knee injuries at the time, and AFL teams had never yet beaten NFL teams. But "Broadway Joe" pulled it off, 16–7.

Some coaches believe that, when teams are evenly matched, winning is ninety percent mental attitude. For this reason, many professional teams now keep sports psychologists on their staffs to help players with their mental attitudes. These professionals emphasize that mental conditioning backs up physical training. Players who imagine themselves in control become more confident and develop

Most football plays are called in the huddle. If the defense looks prepared for the play, however, the quarterback can change it on the line.

a positive self-image. They can worry less about their mistakes by remembering that their coaches make just as many. And those who focus on their moves before and during a game are less prone to injuries because it is dangerous to perform plays without first thinking about them.

GAME TACTICS

A team's tactics are drawn up by the coach and his assistants. College and professional teams have assistant coaches who handle the strategies and tactics for the offensive, defensive, and specialist teams. These are put into a playbook,

JOE NAMATH: MIND OVER BODY

Throughout his career, and even afterward, Joe Namath had to learn to live with pain. During his playing days, he suffered several knee injuries, a broken cheekbone, broken wrist, broken ankle, four torn shoulder ligaments, and one dislocated finger. "Broadway Joe," however, is an extreme example of a football player whose positive outlook allowed him to take the field despite his injuries and numerous operations on his knees. "He went through more pain than anybody," said his former Jets teammate Jim Hudson. "He played with pain when other guys wouldn't have thought about doing it." Hudson added that every player on Namath's Jets team needed at least one knee operation.

The famous quarterback has remained cheerful after retirement, despite the aftereffects of his injuries, including arthritis that has caused him pain for more than thirty years. In 1992, he had knee replacement surgery that let him walk without pain for the first time in twenty-seven years. "I plan to be around until I'm about 100," he said.

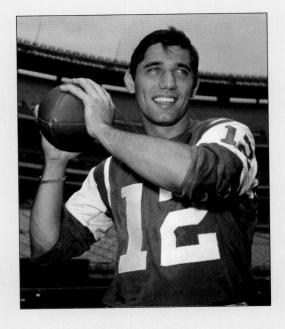

Joe Namath played under "Bear" Bryant at Alabama before taking the New York Jets to victory in the 1969 Super Bowl.

Here a linebacker successfully outwits the opposing team's defense after the quarterback employed a draw play maneuver to deceive the opponent's linemen.

which is usually different for each opponent. Here are four general tactics familiar to players:

- A fake and cut is when a receiver fakes the pass defender by speeding down the sideline and suddenly cutting inside to the spot where the ball should be thrown. Perfect timing means the receiver's body shields the ball from the defensive man.
- A screen play is a fake run by the quarterback, who then throws a pass to a back or receiver in the backfield. This deception is increased by the screen of running backs.
- A change of play occurs when a play or formation called in the huddle is changed on the line. The center may call a line change if he sees the defense

move, and the quarterback can change the play to take advantage of the defense's formation.

- The draw play involves a quarterback dropping back as if to pass. When this draws in the opponent's linemen, the quarterback hands the ball to a back, who tries to run through the resulting defensive gap. This is a good play to employ to counter a **blitz**.

STRANGE TACTICS AND PLAYS

The history of football has included many clever and weird tactics and plays, some of which caused rules to be changed. These include:

- When Jim Thorpe, the great Native American athlete, played for the Carlyle Indian Industrial School, each player in the backfield had a football painted on his jersey and pretended to run with the ball.
- In the 1920s, Notre Dame's coach Knute Rockne introduced "the shift." The backfield took positions arranged as a four-square box, then shifted into a single or double wing before the snap. Until it was banned, this often drew the defense offside.
- Legendary coach Vince Lombardi once changed the numbers of the jerseys of his Green Bay Packers to confuse coach George Hallas and his Chicago Bears.
- In the 1950s, the Army's offensive team would have a player run off to the sideline. The defense thought he was leaving the field, but the "lonesome end" would stay just inbounds and, unguarded, go out for a pass.

Warming Up and Conditioning to Avoid Injuries

Vigorous blocking and tackling makes football the most dangerous team sport, so players must be especially strong, physically fit, and mentally tough. Many football injuries can be prevented, or their effects made less serious, by proper warm-ups.

A warm-up decreases the risk of injury because it stretches the muscles, **ligaments**, and connective tissues; raises the temperature of the muscles and makes them more supple; and increases the heart and respiratory rates, providing more oxygen to your system.

Warm-up sessions should involve only light or moderate exercise, never an exhausting workout that causes you to strain. In a warm-up, you are preparing your body to handle the special energy demands of a game. A warm-up will make the body more flexible and increase its ability to respond more quickly. Another benefit is that it will give you stamina over a longer period, for most injuries occur later in a game when fatigue sets in.

Stretching is one of the best ways to loosen up before a game because this exercise reduces muscle tightness and increases the body's flexibility.

Part of the pregame warm-up is done in unison, such as this stretching exercise for the knees and ankles. The risk of injury is lessened by this activity.

A gradual warm-up of about ten to fifteen minutes (or up to thirty minutes in cold weather) is needed to prepare yourself for a game as vigorous as football. One part of the warm-up is normally a relaxed practice session, as when quarterbacks toss passes to receivers, members of the specialist team sprint, or a place-kicker and holder practice field goals. Warm-ups also include group **calisthenics** such as push-ups, sit-ups, and knee bends. Some teams add alertness drills, moving their hands, legs, and upper bodies quickly in unison.

A good position to begin a warm-up is lying down, so you can gradually warm up the joints of your ankles, knees, and hips. This will make it easier to begin the standing

WARM-UP GUIDELINES

To gain the most benefit from warm-ups, follow a few basic principles:

1. Begin warming up with a light exercise that benefits the whole body. Try jogging or light running.

2. Choose the exercises that will warm up those muscles needed for your game position.

3. Give special time and attention to any parts of your body that have a tendency to be tense or injured.

4. Practice game activities as part of your workout.

5. Maintain an attitude of "relaxed attention," and take this with you into the game.

6. Warm up just before the game. Of course, officials decide this timing for school and professional contests, but you can control the timing for informal games.

7. Increase the time of a warm-up in winter, when muscles are cold and therefore more contracted.

8. Do not warm up for so long or so vigorously that you become fatigued.

Warm-up exercises are also done before football practice sessions.

calisthenic exercises, such as knee bends, running in place, and jumping jacks. The best overall exercise is stretching, which increases your body's flexibility, feels good, and is relaxing. If a football player has too little flexibility, he can suffer muscle strains, pulls, or even tears. Pregame stretching makes the muscle tissues less tight and even a bit longer. Cold muscles resist stretching, so a pregame warm-up should begin with a little light exercise, as when players jog or pitch the football back and forth.

EXERCISES FOR FLEXIBILITY

Some general flexibility exercises are continuous motions; others involve stretching a muscle and holding the stretch for a few seconds.

- **Shoulders, chest, and arms:**
  1. Stretch the arms upward and backward.
  2. Stretch the arms straight up, reaching for the sky one at a time.
  3. Rotate the arms forward in circles on either side, with one moving up as the other descends.
  4. Hold each elbow behind the head in a pulling motion.
  5. Raise the arms to shoulder level, pulling them back, and holding the position.
- **Waist:** Hold the arms out to the side and swing them as you twist the body back and forth.
- **Back, abdomen, and hip muscles:** Lie flat on your back; bend your knees toward your chest and cycle in the air as if riding a bicycle.
- **Lower back and thighs:** Touch your toes, either from a standing or sitting position.
- **Hips and hamstrings:** Sit with the legs spread out and knees locked. Then bend forward and try to grasp each ankle in turn, holding the position for ten seconds.
- **Knees and ankles:** Lie down and alternately bring each knee toward the chest five times, holding the position as you slowly rotate the foot.

Pregame warm-ups prepare a player's body for rough hits and quick responses. More vigorous calisthenics follow the initial stretching exercises.

Although football games exercise all muscle groups, each player should also stretch those muscles most used during a game—a quarterback on his throwing arm, shoulders, and legs; a lineman on his neck, back, and legs.

After a game, a gradual cooling down period of two to five minutes will help your heart and body slow down and return to normal. This is why runners who complete an exhausting race continue to jog lightly. The sore or stiff feeling after a football game is a result of too much blood in the muscles that worked too hard on the field to pump blood back to the heart. A mild type of walking or stretching will help the recovery process. Do not sit down immediately after the game ends, as this can produce a faint feeling.

INJURIES PREVENTED BY WARM-UPS

Simple warm-up exercises can diminish the chances of suffering a painful injury. The following are the most frequent football-related injuries, accompanied by the appropriate preventive exercises:

- Ankle sprains—these range from simple sprains and having a stretched ligament to the more severe sprains that tear a ligament. Do foot rotations.

- Hamstring sprains or pulls—stretch by grasping the ankles while you are sitting.

- Knee injuries—ligaments are stretched and damaged or the kneecap is dislocated. Try the bicycle exercise: lie on your back, cycling.

- Hip pointers—bruising in the hip area. Stretch by grasping the ankles while sitting.

- Back injuries—sprains, bruises, strains, and fractures. Limber up by touching your toes.

- Shoulder injuries—in particular, a separated shoulder, which is a ligament tear, or a dislocated shoulder. Stretch by holding your arms behind your head.

- Stingers—the nerves in the neck are stretched, causing numbness and pain. Stretch by raising or pulling back your arms.

OFF-SEASON FITNESS

Maintaining a regular conditioning program throughout the year is an excellent way to avoid injuries. Strength conditioning is a player's insurance against dangerous

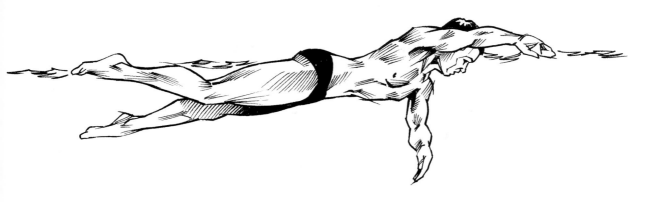

An overall fitness program off-season can include swimming, bicycle riding, jogging, running, and other competitive sports such as tennis and basketball.

fatigue, although heavy weight training should be avoided in the teenage years when the body is still growing. Off-season fitness can be maintained by general exercises, such as running, swimming, or cycling. Tennis, basketball, and other competitive sports can also be an enjoyable way of staying fit. These recreational exercises are aerobic, which means that they improve the way your body takes in oxygen to condition the heart and lungs and produce fuel for the muscles.

As the football season approaches, players should work on conditioning exercises that emphasize strength, speed, and endurance, paying special attention to the muscle groups most used in games. Pre-season workouts could involve pull-ups and sprinting. The Pop Warner Football program, an organization of some 5,000 teams for youths aged five to sixteen, requires a player to have fifty hours of training and conditioning before playing his first game.

Football players should also avoid over-training, which often happens as the football season begins. Symptoms of over-training include stress on the body and excess tiredness. Poor performance is another sign. These problems are normally temporary and can be reversed, but it is best to avoid them.

Equipment

Even the best-conditioned and most highly skilled athletes need protective equipment to play football. The game could not exist as we know it without helmets and pads, which offer the protection needed against the game's rough bodily contact at high speeds. This protection is expensive, with some colleges spending more than fifteen hundred dollars to outfit each player.

Head injuries, such as a concussion, can be especially dangerous, so much thought has gone into designing the best protective helmets. Extra facial protection can be attached to the helmet in the form of a mouthpiece to protect the teeth. There are also jaw pads, and face masks that shield a player's face from elbows, shoes, and helmets.

Many pads exist for the upper body, which has several fragile areas. The neck roll is a foam-padded collar, usually 1–3 inches (2.5–7.5 cm) thick, which fits around the back of the neck. This protects against a blow that could jolt the head backward and cause **whiplash**, injuring muscles and **vertebrae**. Shoulder pads, which are worn beneath the jersey and give players a broad-shouldered and powerful look, are vital because many tackles and other hits are made with the shoulders. Their plastic shell is underlined with foam and cloth padding, which absorbs much of the shock of a hit and diverts part of the shock away from the point of impact. The pads, which are secured with buckles and snaps, also fit over

A player takes a break from the rough-and-tumble action on the field. His expensive protective equipment and padding is not as heavy and restrictive as it looks.

A football player's upper body protection of helmet and shoulder pads help to shield him from the dangers of jarring trackles and hard falls.

the chest and rib area. The quarterback, as well as players with rib injuries, often wears a flak jacket extension below the pads, and linemen might wear a flap which covers the edges of the pad so that opponents cannot hold onto them. Sometimes the shoulder pads also include a neck roll.

An additional item sometimes worn beneath the jersey is a padded shirt. The padding, usually $1/4$ inch (6 mm) thick, provides protection for the ribs and spine and helps prevent shoulder separations and **stingers**.

Other upper-body protections are upper and lower arm guards, elbow pads, and hand guards. Receivers also wear special "tact gloves" with sticky rubber

SHOE CHOICES

Shoes are the only football equipment to have recognizable brand names. Not only do individual players sign up to wear brands such as Nike or Reebok, but whole teams also have contracts. Shoes come in different versions for artificial turfs and weather conditions. Fans seldom realize that a team may change shoes several times, sometimes in one game.

Cleats, also called spikes, are hard plastic pieces on the bottom of the shoe that dig into the turf. Cleats help players keep their footing and avoid injuries, such as sprains and muscle tears. A common shoe has seven cleats.

The best shoes for natural grass fields have premolded cleats (the most comfortable), or cleats that can be screwed on, which are the best for quick changes in case the weather and field conditions alter. Professional teams use electric cleat drivers. The length of the cleats depend on the conditions.

Artificial turfs require shoes with premolded cleats and the least soles possible, but this varies with the weather.

palms, and linemen wear padded gloves to protect their fingers and hands.

Protection is just as vital for the lower body, with pads worn in pockets inside the tight football pants. These include the essential knee and thigh pads made of vinyl foam and coating, which come in different styles. Players who have been injured can be fitted with the style that best protects the injured area.

Other protective devices include shin guards and jockstraps, as well as a

HELMET DESIGN

Football helmets have to fit perfectly. A player's head must always be measured accurately and the correct size of helmet chosen. Padding, usually of foam rubber, is added for a more secure fit. Professional teams often use air pads that are inflated by a hand bulb on two points of the helmet.

Jaw pads—often mistaken for ear pads—are attached to the helmet to cushion the jaw and keep the lower part of the helmet snug against the player's face. The helmet's chin strap, available in some six versions, adds even more security. The plastic mouthpiece, which looks like a half-moon, can either be loose or attached to the helmet, depending on preference. It is fitted to the player's mouth by being softened in warm water. The player then bites down to leave the imprint of his teeth in the soft plastic. When the plastic cools, this imprint becomes permanent.

The face mask comes in about fifteen different styles to match a player's position and preference.

A face mask is a vital protection against serious damage, but also gives a player good visibility.

"girdle." The girdle is a pair of nylon or polyester shorts that compresses the thighs and buttocks. Connected to it are foam tailbone pads and hip pads, which protect both the hips and pelvic bones from the shock of falling.

MAINTENANCE

All protective equipment must be carefully maintained and stored to keep it in good shape. College and professional teams have equipment managers to stock, fit, clean, repair, transport, and generally keep track of the equipment. (Equipment managers usually major in sports management at college.) Any player can profit by imitating the neat storage habits of these specialists. Uniforms are kept on racks, shoes stacked in their boxes on shelves, smaller items such as chin straps and mouth guards are in plastic containers, and other pieces such as helmets, belts, protective pads, and girdles are kept in open cubbyholes, along with game bags for upcoming trips. Damaged or poorly maintained equipment can cause trouble and even serious injury. A broken chin strap may cause a helmet to come off during a dangerous play. Face masks are often damaged and need replacing. Shoe laces can break, and cleats may need to be repaired, replaced, or just tightened. And all of these jobs are in addition to keeping your uniform clean and crisp.

A football uniform should be carefully measured for each player to ensure comfort and mobility.

Common Injuries and Treatment

"Football is not a contact sport," said Vince Lombardi. "Kissing is a contact sport. Football is a collision sport." So players do expect some aches and pains from the game, but generally they can avoid severe injuries. Even so, every year in the United States there are more than 448,000 football injuries to players under the age of fifteen.

Although the highest rates of injury occur in professional football, young players have special problems. They are still growing, which causes stress on their bones, muscles, **tendons**, and ligaments. Players in grade school seldom suffer bad injuries because they are smaller and slower, but participants in high school are larger, stronger, and faster, which can lead to major injuries in this hard-hitting sport. Very few injuries on the field are fatal, but during the 2001 season in the United States there were seven fatalities in high school football and one in the Pop Warner program.

Injuries are divided into two general types: acute and overuse. An **acute traumatic injury** results from a forceful impact during a game, such as receiving a cross-body block. Such injuries include:

- **contusions**—bruises caused by a direct hit, which may result in swelling and bleeding in the muscles or other tissues;

Football is a hard-hitting collision sport — even the best protective equipment cannot prevent some injuries.

An injured player has quick medical assistance waiting on the sidelines. For serious injuries, coaches and trainers can summon paramedics on call at a stadium.

- sprains—stretches or tears of a ligament, which is the tissue that supports joints by connecting bones and cartilage;
- strains—stretches or tears in a muscle, or in a tendon, which is the tough end of a muscle that connects it to the bone;
- **abrasions** and lacerations—abrasions are scrapes; lacerations are cuts to the skin and are normally deep enough to need stitches;
- **fractures**—the cracking, breaking, or shattering of a bone.

An **overuse injury**, also called a chronic injury, comes from repeating the same action over and over. This could happen to a passing quarterback's wrist, a wide receiver's ankle, or a lineman's shoulder. Although the ache of an overuse injury may seem less important than that of an acute injury, a player should seek treatment so that it does not worsen over time.

FOOT AND ANKLE

Injuries to the feet and ankles are common, no matter which position you play. Besides supporting the weight of your body and equipment, your feet take a pounding during a game. A good example is a wide receiver, who continually dashes down the field. Such activity can lead to heel bruises, stress fractures, and ankle sprains:

- Heel bruises occur because players frequently land hard on their heels instead of their toes. This can cause a sharp pain, as if a rock is in the heel of the shoe. Bruises on the rear of the heel can be caused by being kicked. After a game, a player can treat such simple bruises with the **R.I.C.E.** program, which stands for "rest, ice, compression, and elevation." For at

FOOT INJURIES

The top of a player's foot can be injured by tendonitis and contusions (bruises).

Ankle bone: ligaments can be severely overstretched

Extensor muscles can have irritated tendons

Muscle tendons: tight shoes can cause tendonitis

least twenty to thirty minutes, rest the heel, apply ice, wrap a **compression bandage** around it, then elevate the injured area.

- A stress fracture is an overuse injury that causes tiny cracks in a bone's surface. A receiver is a good candidate for a stress fracture in his feet because he frequently jumps for passes and lands hard. The pain of the fracture will build up gradually with longer play and may cause a limp. A doctor should always be consulted, even if a slight pain remains for a few weeks only. The R.I.C.E. program can also be used, but a fracture will heal only with rest.

- A sprained ankle is one of the most common football injuries. It is most often caused when runners or other players quickly change direction, overstretching the ligaments on the outside of an ankle. As ligaments can take time to heal, a player may find that the sprain reoccurs later in the season. The chances of this happening will be reduced when a player follows his doctor's recommended rest period and rehabilitation exercises.

The R.I.C.E. treatment should begin immediately, and the ankle's inflamation and swelling will usually end after about three days. The ankle can then be gently exercised by rotating it. R.I.C.E. can be used several times a day, and an ankle brace or tape may be applied. A serious sprain should be taped by the team trainer or a doctor. After the swelling goes down, other exercises, such as walking, can then begin.

KNEE AND LEG

Football plays often put too much stress on the knees and legs. Many injuries occur during tackling, especially when kickers, wide receivers, and other players have their legs "taken out" at mid-stride. Collisions or quick turns can cause common knee injuries such as sprains, strains, and dislocated kneecaps. Leg injuries range from bruises to fractures.

- Knee sprains and strains are common. The knee is sprained when one or more ligaments are stretched or torn. This will cause a popping or snapping sound, as well as deep pain. Hamstring sprains behind the knee are common. A strain involves a partial or full tear of a muscle or tendon. The feeling is the same as a sprain, and there may also be bruising. The standard R.I.C.E. treatment is used, and severe injuries may also require a splint or crutches.

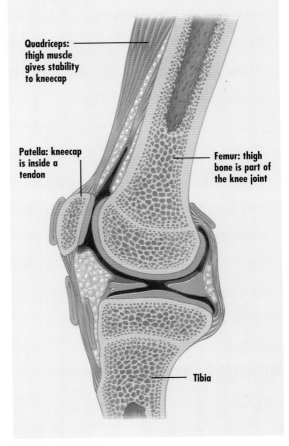

KNEE INJURIES

Injuries to the knee can be painful and often cause a player to miss several games.

Quadriceps: thigh muscle gives stability to kneecap

Patella: kneecap is inside a tendon

Femur: thigh bone is part of the knee joint

Tibia

- A dislocated knee cap, or patella, is one that has been hit off to one side of the knee joint. This can be caused by a hard tackle, and there will be pain and swelling in the front of the knee and a bulge at the side. Even walking will be difficult, and usually a doctor will be needed to put the kneecap back into its proper position. A player can then wear a knee brace to prevent reinjury.

- Leg contusions, or bruises, are common during a game and are often caused by a helmet hitting the front of the thigh. A simple treatment involves applying ice and compression. Stiffness can be prevented by walking or swimming exercises, as stretching the muscle tissue will make it less tight.

- Fractures of the leg make up only about five percent of sports injuries, but a broken leg is painful and can end your season. X rays are needed for correct diagnosis, and either splints or crutches are used, depending on the seriousness of the break.

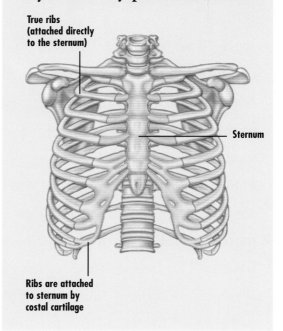

RIB CAGE

A broken rib can be extremely painful; always consult a doctor if you feel any pain in the ribs.

True ribs (attached directly to the sternum)

Sternum

Ribs are attached to sternum by costal cartilage

HIP, RIBS, AND BACK

Injuries to these areas are mostly likely to be bruises and sprains, although hard impact can lead to broken ribs. Quarterbacks often sustain bruised or broken ribs when they are hit broadside as they throw a pass, and wide receivers are in danger when stretching for a reception. Back injuries, often suffered by linemen, are normally just sprains.

- **Hip pointers** are bruises at the upper ridge of the pelvis. You can also strain the adductor muscles under the hips by moving sideways on the field. These problems are treated with ice and protective padding.

- Rib injuries are particularly painful and often require an X ray to determine if there is a break. Taping or a brace might be needed. Even if the fractured rib is not separated (displaced), you should still allow about six weeks of rest in order for it to heal.

- A sprained back can recover if braced, but a severe hit to the back can cause a slipped disk, in which the disk moves out of place. This could put pressure on nerves and cause pain or a pins-and-needles sensation. Treatment includes medication, wearing a neck collar, traction, and sometimes surgery.

- Fractures of the vertebrae also occur after a hard blow or if the back is bent backward. A fracture is rare and can be dangerous, but most back pains are caused by overuse throughout the season. Treatment for overuse injuries may include rest, stretching exercises, and a back support. Recovery usually takes about six weeks. A player with a minor fracture may have to wear a neck brace until the bone heals (six to eight weeks), or, in severe cases, may need traction and surgery.

SHOULDERS, ARMS, AND WRISTS

Both tackling and falling lead to many injuries of the shoulders, arms, wrists, and fingers. Linemen may also be injured as they push across the line. The most serious problems include separated or dislocated shoulders, and broken arms and wrists.

- A separated shoulder is a ligament tear that results in the end of the collar bone (clavicle) raising up slightly. This is usually corrected by a period of rest, followed by strengthening exercises.

- A more serious injury, a dislocated shoulder, involves the shoulder popping out of its socket because of loose ligaments or a torn cartilage. X rays are normally taken in this case, and a shoulder sling is worn for approximately three weeks. Surgery is required only for the most serious dislocations.

A forearm injury, common in football, will heal much quicker under the guidance of a physical therapist.

- A broken arm, wrist, or finger must be treated quickly on the sidelines with a splint, although players have been known to finish a game believing that they have suffered only a sprain. Wrists are very delicate, and sprains are common. Any broken bone must be x-rayed and a cast put in place.

NECK AND HEAD

The most serious football injuries involve the neck and head, so strong protective equipment is worn over these areas. Such injuries are more common when heads are lowered, as when a defensive back makes a tackle, or a running back bends over to protect the ball. Neck injuries range from stingers and whiplash to bruises, sprains, and fractures. Head injuries include concussions, fractures, and **hematomas**.

- A stinger is caused by the nerves of the neck being stretched. This causes a stinging pain and temporary numbness. Although these symptoms will normally go away soon, you should inform your coach or trainer.

AVOIDING HEATSTROKE

Heatstroke is caused by overexposure to heat, leaving the body's heat-regulation system unable to cope with the high temperatures. It may also be caused by overexposure to the sun, in which case it is called sunstroke. Symptoms include a high fever, dry skin, faintness, and collapse. Sometimes, heatstroke leads to convulsions, coma, and even death. From 1960 through 2001, one hundred football players died of heatstroke in the United States. But every case of heatstroke, and the slightly less serious "heat exhaustion," could be avoided by the following precautions:

- Drink cold water regularly.
- Take rest periods in cool areas, removing helmets and loosening or removing jerseys.
- On very hot or humid or days, lower activity levels.
- Be aware of the symptoms of heatstroke, such as flushing, nausea, fatigue, unsteadiness, and vomiting. If any of these symptoms occur, a doctor should be consulted immediately.

Head injuries are always taken seriously in football. Any concussion will require X rays or scans to determine the kind of treatment needed.

- Whiplash is a sprain or strain, caused by the neck being snapped backward. Treatment requires a neck collar or brace.

- A neck fracture or other serious injury may involve the spinal cord. A player on the ground with a neck injury should not be moved before an emergency crew arrives. Movement could cause paralysis and even death. For less serious neck injuries, such as sprains and strains, doctors may rule out further play until symptoms disappear, and the neck is protected with a brace and strengthened by exercise.

- All head injuries are assumed to be serious because a blow to the head can lead to a fatal hematoma, which involves bleeding under the skull. When such bleeding builds up, it causes increasing pressure to the brain. Small hematomas may clear up themselves, but surgery may be required to remove a blood clot. Fortunately, more than ninety percent of concussions are mild, but even mild concussions can cause such problems as headache, lack of alertness, poor even unconsciousness. An athlete should stop playing immediately if he suffers any of these symptoms. X rays will determine the seriousness of the injury. A player should not compete for one to four weeks after the symptoms disappear.

SEEING A DOCTOR

In the case of any serious injury, a player should always inform his coach or trainer, who will insist that he consult a doctor. However, if an injury worsens after the season ends, it may be up to the player to seek medical treatment on his own.

After X rays or scans, your doctor might select simple treatments such as pain relief medicines, rest, and ice packs. For serious cases such as broken bones, you may be given a splint or cast to wear, and may even be advised to have surgery. After this, you may be advised to wear a protective device during play, such as a wrist guard or knee brace; to have physical therapy; or even to stop playing until you heal.

Careers in Football

A good high school football player may be able to join a college team. Even if he attends a small college unable to offer an athletic scholarship, intercollegiate football is enthusiastic and rewarding. And skills developed at small or junior colleges have enabled many players to move up to university or professional teams.

There are more than 75,000 participants on college and university football teams in the United States. The best high school players, of course, are recruited by large universities, which have nationally-recognized programs. A star player may be contacted by thirty or more major schools. These institutions receive television exposure and bowl invitations, which increase their players' chances of rewarding professional careers.

Football scholarships to most four-year colleges and universities are regulated by the National Collegiate Athletic Association (**NCAA**), which also controls recruiting and eligibility. The largest colleges and universities, which are in Division I-A, are each allowed to have eighty-five players on football scholarships. This number allows for three scholarship players for each offensive and defensive position, as well as a punter and a placekicker, with eleven scholarships left over. Major schools with smaller programs are in the NCAA's Division I-AA and are allowed sixty-three scholarships.

Football can be an enjoyable pastime or school sport, and a rewarding career. Professional players have a special dedication to the game that has become their livelihood.

These football awards are highly competitive, and some schools do not use their full number. Only about one in ten high school players who receive a recruitment letter will be offered a full football scholarship. The chances of gaining a scholarship are lower if a high school player has injuries or low academic grades. The lowest accepted high school grade point average (GPA) is 2.0. And even in college, students are required by the NCAA to take certain courses and maintain a minimum GPA to continue playing. This is 1.8 in the freshman year and then rises to 2.0.

Still, you can increase your chances of landing a football scholarship by making a college aware of your abilities on the field. College coaches and scouts attend high school games, but they can hardly be expected to know all the talented players, especially those with specialist abilities. A great many small and private colleges do not even have the funds to visit and recruit players. But you never know when a college coach is in the stands, so always play your best.

This means you must find a way to stand out and impress these important decision-makers. A good starting point is to have your high school coach recommend and promote you

Players who always give their best on the field will soon draw the attention of college and professional scouts in the stands.

Teamwork begins early, as seen in this game between players who are ten to twelve years old. Players who are still growing, however, may risk special injury problems.

Famous college teams such as Notre Dame, whose ball carrier scored a touchdown on this play, are a good stepping stone into the ranks of professional football.

to college recruiters and even arrange tryouts with the coaching staff of the schools you prefer. Ask your coach to phone, giving him the contact name and number, or you can contact a college or university directly. Coaches never mind a phone call from an enthusiastic player, and it helps them reach a decision more quickly. Also, keep them informed of your play during your senior year, especially if you have exceptional games, break records, or if you earn other honors. Be persistent.

Finally, there are professional companies that offer college football placement services, but they normally charge a fee of about $100 to $500. Most have Internet sites that can be found by entering "football scholarships" on a search engine.

THE TOP TEAMS

You may already be familiar with the top football colleges and universities in your region and the nation. Many have a strong tradition of winning, and this attracts the interests of professional teams when they draw up their draft picks from the college ranks. Three of the strongest football programs have been at:

- ALABAMA—the Crimson Tide of the Southeastern Conference has produced twelve national championships and been to more bowls than any school (fifty-

PAUL HORNUNG: KNOWING WHEN TO QUIT

Paul Hornung has been called the best all-around football player to take the field. At Notre Dame during the 1950s, he played quarterback, halfback, fullback, and defensive safety. He was also the team's kicker, handling field goals, punts, and kickoffs. In 1957, this All-American and Heisman Trophy winner was drafted by the Green Bay Packers, for whom he played both quarterback and kicker.

Sadly, Hornung's professional career lasted only nine years because of a series of injuries that began in 1962. Still, he helped "the Pack" win four NFL titles—1961, 1962, 1965, 1966—and led the league in scoring for four years, including a record 176 points in 1960. By 1967, however, a neck injury cost him his only chance to play in the Super Bowl, when Green Bay defeated Kansas City in that first-ever event.

In 1967, Hornung decided to retire rather than risk a serious, permanent injury. He was inducted into the College Football Hall of Fame in 1985 and the Pro Football Hall of Fame in 1986.

MARSHALL FAULK: REFUSING TO QUIT

During the 2000 season, Marshall Faulk, running back for the St. Louis Rams, led the NFL in scoring, with eighty-eight points and fourteen touchdowns. Then doctors confirmed that he had a loose cartilage, bruised bone, and scar tissue in his right knee.

Football is not recommended after a cartilage tear, yet Faulk knew that he had scored his career best of four touchdowns in his last game. He decided to play the rest of the season and was named the league's "Most Valuable Player" for the year.

Faulk had an operation before the next season, and his ability to keep playing despite his injuries has been nothing short of remarkable. In 2001, despite missing two games with a bruised knee, the 28-year-old star led the league. He scored twenty-one touchdowns, ran for 1,382 yards, and caught eighty-three passes for 765 more yards, to become the first player in NFL history to gain at least 2,000 yards from scrimmage in four straight seasons.

Marshall Faulk's twenty-one touchdowns in the 2001–2002 season led the NFL and he was named "Player of the Year" by *The Sporting News*.

one by 2003). Alabama quarterbacks who have gone on to the NFL include Joe Namath of the New York Jets, Bart Starr of the Green Bay Packers, and Ken Stabler of the Oakland Raiders. And don't forget coach Paul "Bear" Bryant.

- NOTRE DAME—the Fighting Irish, an independent team, are America's most famous football name, having won eleven national championships and produced seven Heisman Trophy winners, including Paul Hornung, John Huarte, and Tim Brown. Among their famed coaches are Knute Rockne, Frank Leahy, and Lou Holtz. And the Irish have put more than 400 players into the NFL.

- OKLAHOMA—the Sooners of the Big 12 Conference have won more games since World War II than any team, with 481 victories from 1946 through 2002 (including forty-seven straight wins). They had been to thirty-seven bowl games by 2003, when they won the Rose Bowl. Their many winning coaches, such as Bud Wilkinson and Barry Switzer, have taken them to seven national championships.

These teams are just three of the many winning programs available in the United States. There are nearly 200 schools in the NCAA's Division I. The successful ones are too numerous to list completely, but include Auburn University, Arizona State University, Florida State University, the University of Georgia, the University of Miami (Florida), Miami University (Ohio), the University of Michigan, the University of Nebraska, Ohio State University, Penn State University, the University of Southern California, the University of Tennessee, the University of Texas, and the University of Washington.

Among the smaller colleges with excellent football teams are Augustana (Illinois), Dayton, Eastern Kentucky, Georgia Southern, Ithaca, Marshall, Montana, North Alabama, North Dakota State, Northern Colorado, Pittsburg State, and Youngstown State.

Glossary

Abrasion: An injury in which the skin is scraped off.

Acute traumatic injury: An injury caused by a forceful hit.

Blitz: A rush on the passer, by either the linebackers or defensive backs.

Calisthenics: Exercises designed to improve suppleness and balance.

Compression bandage: A bandage that holds a swollen joint or muscle tightly, in order to reduce the swelling.

Contusion: A bruise in which the skin is not broken.

Down: A play made to advance the ball, or the time given for play.

Fracture: A crack, break, or shattering of a bone.

Gridiron: The football field.

Hamstrings: The group of three muscles set at the back of the thigh.

Hematoma: A swelling containing blood which leaks from a blood vessel.

Hip pointer: A bruise at the upper ridge of the pelvis.

Kickoff: When a team begins a play by kicking off to their opponents' area.

Ligament: A short band of tough body tissue, which connects bones or holds joints together.

NCAA: Abbreviation for the National Collegiate Athletic Association, the organization that establishes sports rules and regulations for most four-year colleges and universities.

Overuse injury: An injury caused by repeating the same action many times.

Play: A phase in a football game when the attacking team try to advance ten yards; each team is allowed four plays to make a first down.

Punt: (n.) A kick. (v.) To kick.

R.I.C.E.: An injury treatment program of rest, ice, compression, and elevation.

Stinger: A neck injury in which the nerves are stretched.

Tendon: A body tissue, also called a sinew, that connects muscles to bones.

The Zone: A condition in which the mind and body are working together to accomplish something.

Vertebrae: One of the bony or cartilaginous segments making up the spinal column.

Whiplash: An injury caused by the neck being snapped backward.

Further Information

USEFUL WEB SITES

"Dealing with Sports Injuries" by The Nemours Foundation:

www.kidshealth.org/teen/food_fitness/sports/sports_injuries.html

National Collegiate Athletic Association (NCAA): www.ncaa.org

"A Guide to Safety for Young Athletes," by the American Academy of

Orthopaedic Surgeons: www.orthoinfo.aaos.org

Football safety equipment of the Carolina Panthers: www.roanoke.edu

The Web sites listed on this page were active at the time of publication. The publisher is not responsible for Web sites that have changed their address or discontinued operation since the date of publication. The publisher will review and update the Web sites upon each reprint.

FURTHER READING

Aretha, David. *The Notre Dame Fighting Irish Football Team.* Springfield, New Jersey: Enslow Publishers, 2001.

Crisfield, Deborah. *Sports Injuries.* New York: Crestwood House, 1991.

Knapp, Ron. *Top 10 College Football Coaches.* Springfield, New Jersey: Enslow Publishers, 1999.

Lloyd, Bryant. *Football: Equipment.* Vero Beach, Florida: The Rourke Book Company, 1997.

Prima Games. *NFL Fever 2003: Prima's Official Strategy Guide.* Roseville, California: Prima Games, 2002.

Roberts, R. *Sports Injuries.* Brookfield, Connecticut: The Millbrook Press, 2001.

THE AUTHOR

Dr. John D. Wright is a writer and journalist with many years of experience. He has been a reporter for *Time* and *People* magazines, a journalist for the U.S. Navy, and reported for newspapers in Alabama and Tennessee. He holds a Ph.D. degree in Communications from the University of Texas, and has taught journalism at colleges in Alabama and Virginia. He now lives in Herefordshire, England.

THE CONSULTANTS

Susan Saliba, Ph.D., is a senior associate athletic trainer and a clinical instructor at the University of Virginia in Charlottesville, Virginia. A certified athletic trainer and licensed physical therapist, Dr. Saliba provides sports medicine care, including prevention, treatment, and rehabilitation for the varsity athletes at the University. Dr. Saliba holds dual appointments as an Assistant Professor in the Curry School of Education and the Department of Orthopaedic Surgery. She is a member of the National Athletic Trainers' Association's Educational Executive Committee and its Clinical Education Committee.

Eric Small, M.D., a Harvard-trained sports medicine physician, is a nationally recognized expert in the field of sports injuries, nutritional supplements, and weight management programs. He is author of *Kids & Sports* (2002) and is Assistant Clinical Professor of Pediatrics, Orthopedics, and Rehabilitation Medicine at Mount Sinai School of Medicine in New York. He is also Director of the Sports Medicine Center for Young Athletes at Blythedale Children's Hospital in Valhalla, New York. Dr. Small has served on the American Academy of Pediatrics Committee on Sports Medicine for the past six years, where he develops national policy regarding children's medical issues and sports.

Index

Page numbers in *italics* refer to photographs and illustrations.

American Football League (AFL) 13, 21
ankle injuries 31, 43, 44
arm injuries 47, 48
Astro Turf 14, 16

back injuries 15, 32, 46, 47
Bryant, Paul "Bear" 13, 16–17, 23, 59

career development *52*, 53–9
Chicago Bears *8*, 12
coaches *12*, 13, 16–17, 19, 41, 54, 56
colleges 9, 13, 16–17, 53–4, 56, 57, 59
Crimson Tide 17, 57, 59

dislocations 23, 32, 45, 47, 48
doctors 44, 45, 49, 51, 58

equipment
    face masks 35, 38
    gloves 36–7
    helmets 10, 35, *36*, 38, 39
    maintenance 37, 39
    mouth guards 35, 38, 39
    pads 35–9
    shoes 37, 39
exercises
    after injury 44, 46, 48
    calisthenics 28, 30, *31*
    fitness 32–3
    warming up *26*, 27–32
    see also muscles; preparation

Faulk, Marshall *58*
fields 9, 14, 16, 37
foot and ankle injuries 31, 43–4
football
    history *8*, 9–10, 12–14, 16–17
    rules 9–10, 11, 13–14
    tactics 22, 24–5
fractures 23, 42, 44, 46, 47, 48, 49, 50–1

gloves 36–7
Grange, Red *8*
Green Bay Packers 12–13, 16, 57, 59

Halls of Fame 16, 57

head injuries 35, 48–9, *50*, 51
heatstroke 49
Heisman Trophy 9, 57, 59
helmets 10, 35, *36*, 38, 39
hip injuries 46–7
Hornung, Paul *18*, 57, 59

injuries
    ankles 31, 43, 44
    arms 47, 48
    back 15, 32, 46, 47
    dislocations 23, 32, 45, 47, 48
    feet 43–4
    fractures 23, 42, 44, 46, 47, 48, 49,
      50–1
    head 35, 48–9, *50*, 51
    hips 46–7
    knees 23, 32, 44–5, 58
    legs 44–5, 46
    neck 32, 35, 48–51
    overuse 41, 42–3, 47
    preventing 27–8, 32
    R.I.C.E. treatment 43–4, 45, 46
    ribs 46, 47
    shoulders 32, 47–8
    sprains 32, 42, 44, 45, 46, 47, 48–9,
      50

Kansas City Chiefs 13, 57
knee injuries 23, 32, 44–5, 58

leg injuries 44–5, 46
Lombardi, Vince *12*, 13, 16, 19, 41

mental preparation *18*, 19–22
Montana, Joe 15
mouth guards 35, 38, 39
muscles
    conditioning 32–3
    stretching *26*, 27, *28*, 30–2
    see also exercises; injuries

Namath, Joe 21, 23, 59
National Collegiate Athletic Association
    (NCAA) 53–4, 59
National Football League (NFL) 12, 13,
    21, 58, 59
neck injuries 32, 35, 48–51
New York Jets 21, 23, 59
Notre Dame 10, *56*, 57, 59

overuse injuries 41, 42–3, 47

pads 35–9
pain 44, 45, 49
Philadelphia Eagles 12
physical preparation *26*, 27–33
plays 22, 24–5
positive thinking 19–20
preparation
    mental *18*, 19–22
    physical *26*, 27–33
professional players 12, *52*, 53, 59
    see also National Football League
protective equipment 10, *34*, 35–9, *40*

Rest, Ice, Compression, and Elevation
    (R.I.C.E.) treatment 43–4, 45, 46
rib injuries 46, 47
Rockne, Knut 11, 59
Rose Bowl 9, 59
rules 9–10, 11, 13–14

scholarships 53–4, 56
school football 41, 53–4, *55*, 56
self-confidence 19–21
shoes 37, 39
shoulder injuries 32, 47–8
sprains 32, 42, 44, 45, 46, 47, 48–9, 50
stretching *26*, 27, *28*, 30–2
Super Bowl 12, 15, 16, 21, 57
surgery 47, 48, 51, 58

tactics 22, 24–5

uniforms 10, 39
universities 9, 13, 16–17, 53–4, 56, 57,
    59

visualization 19–20, 21–2

warming up *26*, 27–32

X rays 46, 47, 48, *50*, 51